Life After Death

Scott Petty

Contents

Introduction

Would you ever believe that the devil's real name is Toby? Rowan Atkinson, the British comedian who is best known for playing Mr Bean, does a comedy sketch in which he plays the devil in hell. Amidst swirling smoke on the stage, attired in a dressing gown and surprisingly short horns, Atkinson's devil says he prefers to be known as Toby. The sketch continues humorously as it plays upon some of the well-known, although not necessarily well-researched, features of the afterlife. 'Sketch' is actually a good name for the performance because Atkinson's devil is like a cartoon character. These days it is pretty trendy to make fun of the idea of heaven and hell being real places, and the devil being a real person. Most people only ever visualize the devil and hell in cartoon forms: burning flames, sulphurous smoke and a little red guy with horns and a pointy tail poking people in the butt with his pronged pitchfork.

We're meant to laugh at comedians and get a giggle out of cartoons. But we wouldn't want Mr Bean to be our final authority when it comes to matters as important as life after death. At the end of the day, how can Rowan Atkinson be so sure that heaven and hell are things to be made fun of rather than things to be taken deadly seriously? How does anyone know what happens after you die? How can you ever be sure of what's next? These are all pretty good questions to be asking.

Who can say?

Perhaps the first thing to say on this whole topic is that if we want to be sure of what happens after we die—where we go, if anywhere at all—we need someone who has been there to tell us. Of course when Rowan Atkinson pretends to be Toby the devil, he's not making a serious point that he knows what's going to happen after we die. But plenty of people do think they know what's going to happen. It's not uncommon, as I wrote about in the Little Back Book *God and Science,* for people to hold very firm views that nothing happens after we die; that we simply disintegrate into the atoms that made us—no more, no less; that there is nothing more than the few short decades we have in this world before we become food for worms.

But people with such confidence that nothing happens overlook one key point: they haven't died yet. That is, they haven't experienced what they are so confident about, and they haven't come back to let the rest of us know. For that matter, neither has anyone who believes that heaven and hell are real places. And perhaps that is part of the argument. Who can say anything with certainty about life after death? To be really sure of what happens after we die we need someone who has been there, wherever 'there' might be, to come back and tell us what it's really like. But nobody has ever done that. Except the person at the centre of the Scriptures: Jesus Christ.

In John's Gospel (one of the biographies of Jesus' life), there's a section that records Jesus talking to a Jewish religious official called Nicodemus. Nicodemus is having real difficulty understanding what Jesus meant when he said that you need to be born again to have eternal life. Fair enough—like many of the things Jesus says in John's Gospel, it's not the most straightforward way of putting things. But as Jesus tries to explain this spiritual concept to Nicodemus, look at what he says:

"I have spoken to you of earthly things and you do not believe; how then will you believe if I speak of heavenly things? No-one has ever gone into heaven except the one who came from heaven—the Son of Man." (John 3:12-13)

If you want someone to speak with certainty about things beyond this life, heavenly things, they will only have credibility if they come from heaven. And Jesus, the Son of Man, says that he's the only one who can speak with credibility and certainty about such things because he's the only one who has been there. Comedians, Christians and atheists cannot speak from their own authority on these things. If we want to know about life after death, if we want certainty about something like heaven, we need someone who has been there to tell us about it. Jesus is that person. In actual fact Jesus doesn't just *tell* us about heaven and eternal life; he clearly says that he is *the way* to heaven and eternal life.

But for now we're just going to pause to note that when we listen in to Scripture's discussion of life after death and things eternal, we're not making things up in our head. We are listening to the one who came from heaven, who passed through death and lives forevermore—Jesus. So what does Jesus say about eternal life, and what will Jesus do to bring it? That's what this little book is all about.

CHAPTER 1

Jesus' resurrection

Think about this: if you were to visit the Queen of England, would you dress up for it? Would you put on your best clothes? Would you maybe even buy some new clothes? Or would you rock up to the Queen's palace in your track pants and joggers, or boardshorts and flip-flops? I ask that question because every time I have ever seen people meet the Queen on television, and even the time I went to her palace in London, people get dressed up, try to clean themselves up, try to look their best. It seems to me that when we go to the palace to visit the Queen, we try to make ourselves look good. So you might expect that if we want to stand before the throne of God, and to have eternal life with him, surely we would need to make ourselves look good for God, or make ourselves be good enough for God. But Jesus says the route to eternal life—or life after death, or heaven,[1] or whatever you want to call it—is different. Just a little further along in the conversation we eavesdropped on earlier, Jesus says that he is the way to eternal life:

> "…the Son of Man must be lifted up, that everyone who believes may have eternal life in him."
>
> For God so loved the world that he gave his one and only Son, that whoever believes in him shall not perish but have eternal life. (John 3:14-16)

In other words, Jesus doesn't just affirm that life beyond this life is real; he clearly says that he is the way to get there. Heaven, or eternal life as he calls it here, is connected to belief in Jesus. In fact it is not just connected to Jesus; it is only available at all on account of Jesus' death in our place. That's what he means when he says that "the Son of Man must be lifted up". He is saying that he must be raised onto a cross in the place of sinful people, like you and me, to die for them so that they might have eternal life. When he says that "God so loved the world that he gave his one and only Son", it means that God gave his Son up unto death. That's an extraordinary statement to make. But eternal life is only available because Jesus—the Son of Man, the Son of God—died in our place to make it available. And because its availability only comes through Jesus then it is our belief or trust or allegiance or loyalty to him that matters most, not how good we are at cleaning ourselves up before God. Now when I say 'belief', it's more than saying "I think Jesus is true"; it's more than intellectual agreement. It is belief that says, "I will trust that Jesus' death has paid for my past, present and future sins. I entrust my present, my future and my eternity to him, and I will follow him as Lord, boss and master of my life, all the days of my life." It's belief with backbone; a wholehearted loyalty to Jesus. But it is belief; it's not trying to be good enough.

Have you ever wondered whether it would make a difference if Jesus died and stayed dead? If he had to be lifted up onto a cross to secure salvation and forgiveness for us, does it matter if he doesn't rise again? Hadn't the hard work been done by the time Jesus died; hadn't the price been paid? Isn't Jesus' *death* really the priority of the whole Christian message and faith? This question of priority is an interesting matter in life in general, because how we prioritize our time and our money and our energy really makes up our life.

I've become a fan of those 'de-motivational' posters you see around the place. There used to be a whole lot of 'motivational' posters, with inspiring scenes from nature and bold words written underneath like 'attitude', 'perseverance', 'commitment', and things like that. But then a whole lot of people started ripping motivational posters off, so that de-motivational posters are now much more popular, which I think is altogether much better. There are some classic de-motivational posters, like the picture of the boy whose head is being bitten by an alpaca while his dad gets the perfect snapshot of it. And there's the new mother who's updating her Facebook status and Twitter feed before she holds her freshly born baby for the first time.

But one particular de-motivational poster caught my eye recently. In front of a crumpled car that is balancing on its roof at the side of a busy road is the driver, an attractive woman. But she's not assessing the situation for further danger or making sure that she hasn't suffered internal bleeding or a head injury, which would be a reasonable expectation given the damaged state of her upturned jalopy. Instead she's brushing her strikingly blonde hair to make sure she looks just right. So getting the perfect picture takes priority over rescuing your son from a hungry alpaca, and updating social media takes priority over holding your baby as it draws its first breaths. And looking good is the most important response to a life-threatening accident. Interesting priorities. But when the apostle Paul, one of Jesus' specially appointed spokesmen, thinks about what is of first importance to the Christian message, and what the priority of the gospel is, he doesn't focus on Jesus' death alone. He also focuses on Jesus' resurrection. Look at what he says to the Corinthian Christians:

> For what I received I passed on to you as of first importance: that Christ died for our sins according to the Scriptures, that he was buried, that he was raised on the third day according to the Scriptures, and that he appeared to Cephas, and then to the Twelve. After that, he appeared to more than five hundred of the brothers and sisters at the same time, most of whom are still living, though some have fallen asleep. Then he appeared to James, then to all the apostles, and last of all he appeared to me also, as to one abnormally born. (1 Cor 15:3-8)

When the apostle Paul thinks about what is of first importance to Christian belief, he says it is nothing other than the death of Jesus "for our sins", as we've already discussed. But notice that he really majors on the resurrection. The priority, the matter of first importance, is not only Jesus' death but also his resurrection (as evidenced by many appearances after he rose from the dead).

Paul wants us to know that the resurrection amazingly,

extraordinarily, certainly and really happened. Jesus died for our sins, according to the Scriptures. But he then really rose from the dead, also according to the Scriptures. I guess that's the point of Paul telling us about all the people who saw Jesus after he died and rose again to life. Look at what is an impressive list of people:

- After Jesus was raised on the third day he appeared to Peter, the chief disciple, leader of the gang.
- Then he appeared to the Twelve (which is code for the remaining disciples).
- Then he appeared to more than 500 people at the same time. And most of those 500 were still alive at the time Paul wrote 1 Corinthians.
- Then he appeared again to the apostles.

In other words, Paul is saying to his first readers that if they doubt that Jesus really rose from the dead, they can go and ask one of the people who saw him. Or they can go and ask a hundred of the people who saw him. There were more than 500 to choose from, although a few may have died (or "fallen asleep", as verse 6 nicknames physical death) in the time between. They would testify that they saw the crucified Christ risen from the dead. I don't think anybody need ask you to believe in Christ Jesus without suitable evidence; Paul certainly doesn't require people to make the gospel their priority without plain and abundant reason. There were over 500 people who saw the resurrected Jesus at the same time, showing that the resurrection really happened.

And that is so significant because the resurrection of Jesus is the thing that allows us to affirm everything that Jesus said about himself. The resurrection gives us confidence to say that Jesus was himself God; that he was sent by God; that he conquered death; and especially that his death paid the penalty our sins deserve. Or to put it the other way around: what could we actually say if Jesus never rose from the dead? Nothing, I think. Nothing; he's just another guy who thought he was special but who died, and that's not special at all. He's just another lunatic who claimed to be God, who died, proving precisely that he was not God. But the resurrection changes everything, because the resurrection proves that everything he said about himself was true. Only because of the resurrection can we actually say that Christ died for our sins. The resurrection really happened. If you were around at the time you could have asked about 500 people who saw Jesus with their own eyes after he rose from the dead.

His resurrection guarantees our 'next'

The astounding thing is not only that Jesus' resurrection is real, which means we can believe with confidence; it's that Jesus' resurrection guarantees *our* resurrection. Or to put it more simply, Jesus' resurrection guarantees us our 'next', our future. In the subsequent verses of chapter 15 in 1 Corinthians, the apostle Paul outlines all the problems that flow if you don't believe the resurrection of Jesus, that most important piece of the whole gospel of Christ. If Christ has not been raised then the apostles' preaching was useless and our belief is useless. If Christ has not been raised from the dead, the apostles were liars and Christians are losers ("of all people most to be pitied" is how Paul describes us in verse 19) and, even worse, still lost in our sins. If Christ was not raised from the dead then our hope is only for this life, and that's a ridiculous situation because we're losers now and lost for all eternity. Without the historical resurrection we have no next. And that explains why Paul's bold assertion in verse 20 sounds so sweet:

> But Christ has indeed been raised from the dead, the firstfruits of those who have fallen asleep. (1 Cor 15:20)

Jesus has indeed been raised from the dead, says the apostle Paul with conviction. Jesus is alive and that guarantees his followers that they will have a next, a future. Those who have already died ("fallen asleep") will have a next. All those who belong to Jesus will have life beyond death.

Jesus is described as "the firstfruits", which is an odd thing for our modern ears to hear. We don't really come across the concept of firstfruits very much these days because milk doesn't come from cows, fruit doesn't come from trees, and bread doesn't come from grain. Everything comes from the supermarket. That's the place where things grow as far as most city-dwellers are concerned. I once heard that the average age of an apple you buy from the supermarket is 9 months; it sits in cold storage for 9 months. But before food 'grew' in supermarkets, people lived off the land. Milk came from cows, fruit came from trees, and bread was made from stuff that comes out of the ground, commonly known as wheat. Farmers would work hard during the sowing season preparing their fields and sowing the grain or tending their trees. And then they would watch with great eagerness and impatience, waiting for the first heads of wheat to burst through the soil, or waiting for the first buds of fruit to form on the branches.

And when those firstfruits were ripe and ready for harvest it was a great day because that guaranteed that the rest of the harvest would follow. The firstfruits were the guarantee that a harvest full of grain or fruit was on its way. So when the apostle Paul says that Jesus' resurrection is the firstfruits, he is saying that Christians' resurrection from the dead is guaranteed. There is life beyond this life, life beyond the grave. It is inevitable, it is certain, it will happen. We will have a future. We will have our next. So it is not only Jesus' death that counts; his resurrection from the dead is the historical event that paves the way for us to rise from physical death to life eternal.

His resurrection changes our present

But here's the thing: Jesus' resurrection not only guarantees our next, our future—it also changes our present.

This is really important because a lot of people today live like the present is all there is. Life is short—too short to drink bad wine, so the saying goes. We're urged to sing like no-one is listening and dance like nobody is watching. I reckon only good singers and dancers say stuff like that because whoever made that up obviously hasn't heard me sing or watched me dance. You may not think about the next; you may not think beyond Friday's party, or Saturday's game, or October's exams, or December's holiday. And it's not just young people who seem trapped in the present. Previously, one generation of parents would work hard and save hard because they wanted to leave their children and grandchildren with an inheritance. They wanted to pass a wad of cash on to the next generation to make it easier for them to own a home or just get ahead on some of the expenses of raising a family. But these days, in my country at least, older generations want to burn through all their cash, buying brand new caravans and Winnebagos and doing lap after ridiculous lap of the continent. They don't really care whether or not there's any money left to give their children.

And if Jesus has not been raised from the dead, if there is no next, that's exactly what they should be doing. Living for the moment. Even the apostle Paul says that "if the dead are not raised"—if we have no future—then "let us eat and drink, for tomorrow we die" (v. 32). Isn't that the motto for our age? Let us eat, drink, sing, dance, play, travel, for tomorrow we die. It's the motto for people who have no hope beyond this life. It's the motto for those without a next. It might even be your motto.

Is it the best motto though? Because Jesus was raised from the dead, and because his followers will follow him in resurrection from death, Paul has a different motto for Christians in the final verse of 1 Corinthians 15:

> Therefore, my dear brothers and sisters, stand firm. Let nothing move you. Always give yourselves fully to the work of the Lord, because you know that your labour in the Lord is not in vain. (v. 58)

In this conclusion to his whole study of the resurrection the apostle Paul returns to where he started at the very beginning, talking about standing firm and letting nothing move those who trust in Christ. People who have a hope beyond the grave, a next, are to stand firmly in that hope, letting nothing move them. Hold firm, stand firm, be reminded, let nothing move you. That's a message each Christian needs to hear every day of the few years God gives us on this earth.

Of course you might think that all sounds a bit passive and defensive. So if you're a bit of a front-foot player—someone who prefers to play offence—and you are after something a bit more active, then take another look at that last sentence: "Always give yourselves fully to the work of the Lord, because you know that your labour in the Lord is not in vain". Doing the work of believing, encouraging, proclaiming and living out the good news of Jesus will look different for each one of us. And it might look different for you next week or next year than it does right now. But there is work in the Lord to be done—the work of believing in Jesus and living it out in all parts of your life; of encouraging others to believe in him, and proclaiming the great news of his death and resurrection to a world that's living for the present. That really is labour that is not in vain; that really is work that is worthwhile; that really is something that will last. The question is whether you're going to be a part of it. The motivation is the knowledge that Jesus' resurrection guarantees our future, our next. The truth is that the historical resurrection of Jesus is at the heart of the good news of salvation in Jesus. And the challenge is to make that good news the priority on which you stand firm and hold firm throughout the days of this life and into eternity, rather than just living for today.

This might of course raise several questions. Like, for how long do I need to stand firm? If Jesus' resurrection guarantees my resurrection to eternal life, exactly what happens to me when I die? And what is left for Jesus to do now that he has been raised from death to life? These penetrating questions are where we turn next.

You might naturally be most concerned with what happens to

us beyond this life. Take a deep breath—we'll get to that matter soon—but the subject of Jesus' return is important to understand first, before we get to what happens to us. Without the return of Jesus it might just seem like life and everything as we know it just goes on and on.

CHAPTER 2

Jesus' return

In the last chapter we discovered how Jesus' resurrection was of first importance to the Christian gospel and faith. Jesus really rose from the dead. Some people who might otherwise struggle with that idea can be persuaded of its accuracy by the reports of hundreds of eyewitnesses of the resurrected Christ. But chances are that there are many who still do not believe that Jesus will come back. You could be one of them. Or perhaps you do believe in the return of Jesus, but only somewhere in the deep recesses of your mind because you know that's what you are supposed to believe. It may not be at the front of your mind that Jesus might return before you die. I have a suspicion that most of us don't think there's any real chance he'll return in our lifetime. And perhaps we don't really want him to, at least not until we've travelled around Europe, or fallen in love, or had a family, or seen Taylor Swift in concert. Then again, some of us might be hoping he returns in the next 24 hours, because we have an English assignment or killer report due in the morning. But deep down, we don't really expect him to return, and we don't really want him to return either, if we're honest.

Definitely coming back...

One thing that is super clear in the New Testament is that Jesus will come to Earth again. He really will. All the New Testament authors—every single one—speak about the coming of the Lord with conviction. So what do they say? They say that Jesus' return, or what Christians sometimes call his 'second coming', will be personal and physical, it will be visible and it will be glorious.

It will be unquestionably personal and physical. It's not like he's just going to somehow return in our hearts or warm our souls or come spiritually into the lives of believers (in fact he already did that when he gave his Holy Spirit as a gift to all believers after he left). Rather, Jesus will return personally and physically. At the start of the New Testament book of Acts, Luke records the scene where Jesus is leaving this world, ascending back to heaven. As the disciples are watching him motor on up, two angels appear beside them. They sort of box the poor disciples around the ears, saying to them:

"Men of Galilee, why do you stand here looking into the sky? This same Jesus, who has been taken from you into heaven, will come back in the same way you have seen him go into heaven. (Acts 1:11)

"Don't look up boys," the angels are effectively saying to them, "there's work to be done spreading the good of Jesus to the whole world. But we do want you to know that Jesus will return. The same Jesus; in the same way; from heaven." Jesus' return will be personal and physical. It will be him coming down from heaven.

And because it's the same Jesus coming down in the same way, his coming will be visible as well. In Matthew 24 Jesus talks extensively about what will happen in the lead-up to his coming back to Earth. Naturally, the disciples are pretty inquisitive about it all and they ask Jesus what sign there might be of his coming and of the end of the age. Jesus says to them three times in that chapter not to believe rumours of his return. Many will come claiming to be Christ, he says (v. 5), trying to deceive people. Some will even perform miraculous signs, presumably under the power of the devil (v. 24), to distract people. Some will say Jesus is out in the desert or hiding in an inside room (v. 26). Jesus warns that there'll be plenty of rumours of his return.

When all the Catholic cardinals and bishops met early in 2013 to elect a new pope, a German dude call Ralph tried to sneak his way into one of the most secret meetings on the planet. He dressed up in black robes, put a purple scarf around his waist that was similar to the sashes worn by senior Catholic officials, and he shook hands and chatted with priests and cardinals arriving at the meeting. Ralph introduced himself to reporters as Bishop Basilius and said he was a member of the Italian Orthodox Church, which is a little interesting seeing as there's no such thing as the Italian Orthodox Church. That should have been the giveaway. But security only worked out he was an imposter because his purple sash was too short and he was wearing a black fedora, which is a hat worn more often by jazz musicians than by Catholic bishops. But maybe if he'd had a longer sash and a better hat he could have snuck all the way in…

Jesus anticipated that there would be plenty of rumours that he would sneak his way back to Earth, in hiding or somewhere secluded. But we won't have to wait for a press release or a public announcement to know whether the rumours are true. Jesus' return will be visible. You won't have to guess; you'll know for yourself. Jesus even says that…

"…as lightning that comes from the east is visible even in the west, so will be the coming of the Son of Man." (Matt 24:27)

Jesus' return will be visible. And not just visible, but visibly glorious. That same chapter in Matthew tells us that the sun will be darkened, the moon will not give its light, and the stars will fall from the sky. Those cosmic calamities will be the forewarning of the reappearance of Jesus, when he will come "on the clouds of heaven with power and great glory" (v. 30). So rather than Jesus sneaking back to Earth, the situation will be far more public and clear. It will be obvious to all. You really won't be able to miss the return of Jesus. The whole sky will change, and if you think about it you can see the sky from wherever you happen to be on this beautiful planet of ours. Everyone will see Jesus coming on the clouds with power and great glory.

But when exactly?

So we know that Jesus will return. We have just seen that he will return personally, physically, visibly and with power and great glory such that everyone will know about it and everyone will see it. But that leaves the question of when; when will Jesus come again? Which really is a whole other question. So whilst we can say that Jesus is definitely coming, we also have to say that we don't know when. It actually appears that at least while Jesus was on Earth, even he didn't know the exact time of his return as it was set by God the Father in heaven (see Matthew 24:36-37).

We just don't know definitely when Jesus will return, and at least while Jesus was on Earth he didn't know definitely when either. And so for us this means his return will be unexpected. Jesus himself compared his return to the time of Noah, when Noah was building his boat in the middle of the desert under sunny skies. You can imagine that people would have been mocking Noah, and certainly they were getting on with life—eating, drinking, getting married, and so on. People were just carrying on with life as normal, until the waters came suddenly and unexpectedly and everything changed.

The return of Jesus will happen suddenly and unexpectedly, which means we need to be prepared at all times, and that is precisely the warning Jesus gives us about his return:

"Therefore keep watch, because you do not know on what day your Lord will come… So you also must be ready, because the Son of Man will come at an hour when you do not expect him." (Matt 24:42, 44)

Jesus' return is described in multiple places as being like a thief in the night. That's such a famous little part of Scripture that it has sort of weaved its way into everyday usage. But if you've ever been robbed or had something stolen from you, then you know from experience what that description really means. My family home got broken into a few years ago. It was very annoying because they took everything of value we had, including my computer, my phone, my iPod, some jewellery, my sunglasses—everything of value. They stuffed all my possessions into my backpack—the one I take on eight youth camps each year—and nicked off with that as well. At eight o'clock on a Saturday morning, two blokes (I presume) walked out of my house with the 37-inch flatscreen TV I bought with a cash bonus that our then Prime Minister—called Kevin—gave us to help kickstart the economy after the global financial crisis. I called it my Kevin-37. You'd have thought someone might notice two blokes walking out of my house in broad daylight with a Kevin-37 flatscreen TV.

A thief in the night has an extra advantage—darkness. You don't know when he's coming and you can't see him going. If you knew when he was coming you'd be ready and waiting to clock him over the head with a piece of metal pipe. Well, I would. But if you don't know when he's coming then you need to be ready or prepared for him to come at any time. We know definitely that Jesus will return; we just don't know with any certainty when that will be, so we need to be prepared at all times.

Getting on with the Christian life

So how do we make sure we are prepared at all times? What does it mean to keep watch or be ready or be prepared for the coming of Christ? This is the money question, because this will affect us in the present, right here, right now.

Jesus tells a number of parables or stories in Matthew 24 and 25 to help us see what it might look like to be ready or to keep watch. And it's different to what some Christians think. There are some Christians who though they are brothers and sisters in Christ, are also pretty much complete nutbars. They scour the internet and newspapers trying to find things in world events and history that reveal when Jesus is going to appear—even though Jesus himself said that no-one will know when it's going to happen until it suddenly and surprisingly takes place for the whole world to see. You might think it's a stretch that such people exist but if you find yourself somehow on their mailing lists as I have, you'll have no doubts. There's actually much more important stuff to be doing to prepare for Jesus' return than scouring the internet or sending newspaper clippings to frustrated pastors and ministers. Anyway, these three or four little stories reveal that we prepare for Jesus' return by wholeheartedly getting on with the Christian life.

There's a familiarity to the parables Jesus tells in this section. In the first one, Jesus says you want to be a faithful and wise servant who is getting on with the tasks the master has assigned to you. It will be good for such servants when Jesus returns and finds them getting on with things—they'll be commended and rewarded for getting on with the job. What the faithful and wise servants don't want to do is to forget that the master is coming back just because he's been away for a long time, and start beating up their fellow servants or getting drunk and generally carrying on like rugby league players. So Jesus is warning us that while we wait for his return, we should be careful we don't get distracted by all the things of this world, especially the foolishness of sinful things that prevent us from doing what we're supposed to be doing as Christians: believing, loving, obeying, serving.

If you don't know what you're supposed to be doing or how to get on with it, the third little parable or story (traditionally known as 'The Parable of the Talents') reminds us to put whatever gifts, abilities and opportunities we have to work in service of Jesus and his gospel message. You will likely know the story, which is a bit of an expanded version of the first parable I've just mentioned. The master goes away on a long journey and entrusts his three servants with different amounts of money, according to their abilities. In the story, the money is usually called 'talents' (or 'bags of gold') but it doesn't just refer to talents or money or gold. The talents represent any gifts, abilities, possessions and opportunities we have as Christians to serve Jesus. And so the servant with five talents put them to work and gained five more. The one with two talents put them to work and gained two more. But the servant with one talent was lazy and afraid and didn't use what the master had given him at all. The master was happy with the first servant, who started with five and gained five more, saying to him, "Well done, good and faithful servant! You have been faithful with a few things; I will put you in charge of many things. Come and share your master's happiness!" (Matt 25:21).

This is exactly what he says to the second servant, who started with two and gained two more: "Well done, good and faithful servant… Come and share your master's happiness!" (Matt 25:23).

But the third servant gets slammed—not because he only started with one, but because he didn't do anything with what the master had given him.

In many ways, young people can think of themselves not unlike that last servant, believing they're not given all that much in terms of gifts or abilities or possessions or opportunities to serve the master Jesus and work for his kingdom. But it doesn't matter what you've been given; what matters is what you do with it while you wait for Jesus to return. At the very least each person has the gift of his or her life—a precious opportunity to grow in your understanding of Jesus, in your love for him, and in a life that imitates him. So any person, but particularly young people who may think they have little to offer the master, should ask themselves, "Am I being a good and faithful servant with that precious opportunity?" Have you ever asked God to help you learn more, love more, look more like Jesus? Because you don't want to be a wicked and lazy servant who thinks that as long as you turn up to church twice a month, you're ready for Jesus' return.

In our families, be they Christian or non-Christian, we have the chance to live for Jesus, respecting our parents and trying to serve our siblings. In our workplaces we have the chance to live for Jesus, working hard and honouring the right demands of our bosses. In our schools and places of study we have the chance to live for Jesus, to be good servants who stand up for Christ, rather than lazy servants who couldn't be bothered. In our churches we have opportunities to both grow as wholehearted disciples of Jesus, and to use whatever gifts and talents we have for the sake of others. So the question is the same: will you make the most of those opportunities or simply waste them?

We might believe in our heads that Jesus is coming back. But when we don't really want to know about it in our hearts, we place ourselves in a position of danger. That is simply because he *is* returning: definitely, personally, publicly, visibly and powerfully. He won't be sneaking back to Earth in the way that German guy Ralph snuck into the meeting to elect a new pope.

But we just don't know when Jesus will come again. In fact, in three of the parables that Jesus tells in Matthew 24 and 25, there's a reference to it being a long time until he returns. A master goes on a long journey; the bridegroom is a long time coming. So in the long time between the resurrection of Jesus, which we considered in the previous chapter, and the return of Jesus that awaits, let us not lose heart or lose focus. The time is now to use all that he has given us to serve him, so that when he returns we will hear those most beautiful words in our ears: Well done, good and faithful servant. Come and share your master's happiness!

CHAPTER 3

What happens when I die?

In the last chapter we considered the return of Jesus and how to live each day fully prepared for his return. But in the case that you die before Jesus returns, what happens then? That's an honest and reasonable question, even though as a society we are generally uncomfortable with the idea of death. As a rule we don't like talking about it and we don't like thinking about it. And perhaps we try to trick ourselves into thinking that if we don't talk about it and we don't think about it, death might just not happen. At least not to us. Perhaps that's the strategy. Just reflect on how we talk about it. We don't call graveyards 'graveyards' any more; they're called 'cemeteries'. And even the word 'cemetery' comes from the Old English word (via Greek and Latin) for dormitory, the place where people go to sleep. And that's the thing isn't it? People don't die any more—they go to sleep, or rest in peace, or pass away, kick the bucket, go belly up, push up daisies, go six feet under, fall off the perch, give up the ghost, bite the dust. When it comes to the insurance that you take out to pay for expenses when you die, they even call it 'life insurance' not 'death insurance', which is a bit odd.

But it's not just at a community level that we are uncomfortable with the idea of death. Individuals will try just about anything to convince themselves they will live forever, including cosmetic surgery. In the past people who were getting older looked like they were getting older. But now many folks get plastic surgery or Botox injections, because apparently looking permanently startled is preferable to looking old. You used to have a granny who looked like a granny. But these days there's an increasing chance that your granny will have her face filled and smile stretched so that she looks more like the Joker from Batman. All in an attempt to defy time and pretend you're not getting older and closer to death.

Although we can giggle at celebrity attempts to defy ageing by resorting to cosmetic enhancements, in actual fact death is no laughing matter. Anyone who has had someone close to them die will understand that acutely. But Christians need not avoid the topic of death, nor try to escape it by not talking or thinking about it. Death will always remain very sad—even Jesus cried when his friend Lazarus died, even though he was about to raise Lazarus back to life. Yet Christians can approach death with great hope. We need not grieve like those without hope, but that can only happen when we understand what happens when we die.

We may live with him

So the first thing we'd need to say in answering this question— "What happens when I die?"—is that clearly our bodies rot; they disintegrate. At one level, that's a pretty obvious statement to make. When we die our organs start to perish and degenerate almost straight away. And if left alone our bodies will quickly decompose. One thing everybody agrees about is that after the point of death, a body that once was full of life is no longer. It's lifeless and will soon break down into the basic elements from which it was made. And so, if people who don't believe in God think that this is all there is, you can understand their grief at the loss of a dearly loved friend or family member. The body of their loved one will not live again; that person is no more as far as they are concerned.

But the only one who has come from heaven to earth, the only person who has been through death never to die again—Jesus—

says differently. As do his officially appointed spokesmen such as the apostle Paul, in places like 1 Thessalonians 4 and 5:

> …we do not want you to be uninformed about those who sleep in death, so that you do not grieve like the rest of mankind, who have no hope… (1 Thess 4:13)

> For God did not appoint us to suffer wrath but to receive salvation through our Lord Jesus Christ. He died for us so that, whether we are awake or asleep, we may live together with him. (1 Thess 5:9-10)

If we were to travel back to first-century Thessalonica, it seems that the Thessalonian Christians were expecting Jesus to return not that long after he ascended back to heaven. Perhaps they were a little like the disciples, still looking at the sky, anticipating Jesus' hasty return. And when he didn't come back straight away, they got stressed out about their Christian friends who had died, or fallen "asleep" as he calls it here (even the apostle Paul sometimes spoke about death by using polite understatements). Perhaps the Thessalonian Christians who remained alive were worried that their brothers and sisters who had died would miss out on being with Jesus when he returned. So the apostle Paul tells them not to be ignorant and not to grieve without hope.

But why? It is because Jesus' death for us means that we live together with him, whether we are awake (that is, physically alive) or asleep (that is, we have physically died). Either way, we live with Jesus. Even when our body gives way to physical death, we may live on in happy fellowship with Jesus. This means death does not have that same sting for us as it does for those without this future hope, because our souls continue in friendship with Jesus, even though our bodies give way. We may not fully understand how this works, but we can know for certain that we live on with him after our physical bodies die. Elsewhere in the New Testament, the apostle Paul describes us as having already been raised to new life with Christ, at the point of becoming believers (see Colossians 3:1-4, Romans 6:4, Ephesians 2:6). This is a new spiritual life in him that begins when we first trust in him and continues beyond our physical death. However this actually works out, the clear message of the New Testament is that physical death is not the end for believers in Christ; we continue to live with him after our bodies die.

My lovely wife and I lived in London for just over three years. London is a very fine city to live in, and one of the good things about living there is that when choosing where to go on holidays there are so many good options available. Within three hours travelling time you can be anywhere from Ireland to North Africa or Russia, and everywhere in between. Now that I live back in Sydney, which again is a very fine city to live in, the options for holidays are somewhat more limited. You either go a few hours up the coast or a few hours down the coast. That's it. Because if you go a few hours east you're in New Zealand—enough said (although Australians and New Zealanders are usually best mates, we would never admit that to each other, certainly not publicly). And if you go a few hours west you're in outback Australia, which is the world's largest sandpit. So I moan about the lack of holiday options from Sydney compared to the options from London. And whenever I moan about it, my wife reminds me that the grass is always greener somewhere else. You might have heard that saying—'The grass is always greener on the other side'. It's a sort of proverb that means you stupidly think things would be better if you were somewhere else or were doing something else. I always reply that the grass *is* actually greener in England. It's lush and lovely and green there; it's a bit dry and yellow in Australia.

When the apostle Paul in the New Testament book of Philippians thinks about life here on Earth compared to life with

Jesus, he basically looks at this life and says that the grass is greener somewhere else. There is something better than living life here on planet Earth:

> For to me, to live is Christ and to die is gain. If I am to go on living in the body, this will mean fruitful labour for me. Yet what shall I choose? I do not know! I am torn between the two: I desire to depart and be with Christ, which is better by far; but it is more necessary for you that I remain in the body. (Phil 1:21-24)

He's just sort of thinking out loud and he says that if he lives, that's good because he can keep working with the Philippian Christians for their benefit. But to die is somehow gain. He desires to leave this life. Is it because he's having a difficult time and he just wants to escape and plastic surgery was not an option back then? Not likely. It's because when he departs this life he gets to be with Christ. And he says in verse 23 that that's better by far; it's greener grass, so to speak. Eventually, in his little speech to himself, he decides it's necessary to stick around for the sake of the Philippians. But it's clear from this that when we die we get to be with Jesus. And that can only be better than living here, if it happens straight away. There would be no need for Paul to weigh up the two options if he knew that upon his physical death he would lie in the dust of the ground for decades or even thousands of years before he got to be reunited with Jesus upon Christ's return.

Some people think that when Christians die their souls sort of go to sleep for the whole time between their physical death and the return of Jesus. Partly that's because the New Testament uses 'sleep' as a way of describing death. I think the New Testament writers are just using sleep as a metaphor for death because when you are dead it sort of looks the same as when you're asleep—you're lying on the ground motionless. In the same way it uses the picture of being awake to mean being alive. But your soul doesn't sleep for decades or hundreds of years or even thousands of years. You get to be with Jesus from the second you die, from the moment you breathe your final breath. That's why Jesus can say to the criminal on the cross who asks Jesus to remember him in his coming kingdom, "Truly I tell you, today you will be with me in paradise" (Luke 23:43). Not in decades or millennia; but "*today* you will be with me in paradise". Our bodies very well may rot, or be burned up (for those who are cremated upon death), or even eaten up (for those who are lost at sea), but our souls are with Jesus right away.

New resurrection bodies

I consider that to be good news—that at the moment our final breath leaves our body we will be in fellowship with Jesus. But this still leaves the question of what happens with our bodies, if anything, into eternity. Personally, I'm totally unattracted to the idea of spending eternity floating about as a disembodied soul somehow still wearing a dress and playing a harp, although I wouldn't mind having wings for a little bit. But the news is good for the Christian. Not only do our souls stay with Jesus the minute we leave this life physically, but following our physical death, we await a resurrection body after Jesus returns. When Jesus returns, there will be a final judgement (we'll think about this more in the next chapter) after which Christians will receive new resurrection bodies for all eternity. I'm getting a new body and I'm looking forward to it. Our souls will be with Christ after physical death just as they were with Christ before physical death. But when it comes to our bodies, we get new ones. And they will be glorious.

The question of glorious bodies is almost *the* obsession of our world today. Many girls gaze wistfully at the entirely unobtainable look of the women emblazoned on the covers of fashion and gossip magazines. Even these real-life beauties have been airbrushed to perfection so that their glory is absurdly out of reach for every woman. Of course that knowledge doesn't always make us feel any better about our less-than-perfect skin and figures. I'd love to encourage you not to swallow the quiet lies these magazines and pictures tell. If it doesn't sound too much like the sugary sweet lines of a boy-band marketed to pre-teenage girls, women are already beautiful and dearly loved by the God who made them in his image.

When I was growing up I had a picture of a muscleman on my wall. He was buff (which I now think means he was on 'supplements'), he was brown (which I now think means he got a spray tan), and he had veins sticking out everywhere (which even then I thought meant he was a bit of a freak). But I wanted to be like him because I thought he had a glorious body. Strong, powerful, almost indestructible. But I reckon he knew his body would not stay glorious for long. Because if he stopped training in the gym for just a few weeks he would lose close to half his cardio fitness and a stack of muscle mass and tone. And I reckon he also knew that the guys who won body-building competitions were never that old. Very soon his body would be past its prime and on its downward spiral towards death. So he could drink as many of those awful protein shakes as he could stomach. He could down as many expensive supplements as he wanted. And he could train his body to oblivion. But he could not avoid the simple truth that he was always fighting a losing battle.

He was always fighting a losing battle because his body, as indestructible as it seemed to me back then, was still an earthly body. It was splendid in its own way, but still made from the dust of the earth and headed back into the dust of the earth. The great truth for Christians is that after physical death we can look forward to new resurrection bodies. Each will be a glorious, spiritual body. Just as Jesus was raised from the dead and now has a new, improved resurrection body, so will all those who belong to him also receive a new body when he returns. When the apostle Paul describes it to the Corinthian Christians he says it's almost like our original physical body is a seed that is planted in the ground upon death, only to be raised as a glorious spiritual body in the future:

> So will it be with the resurrection of the dead. The body that is
> sown [i.e. our old physical body] is perishable [i.e. it can die], it is
> raised imperishable; it is sown in dishonour, it is raised in glory; it is

sown in weakness, it is raised in power; it is sown a natural body, it is raised a spiritual body. (1 Cor 15:42-44)

The Corinthian Christians scoffed at the idea of being raised back to life. But the apostle Paul tells them they wouldn't have the exact same body that they had in this life. They could look forward to receiving a glorious resurrection body. This is such great news if you've ever felt weak in your body, sick in your body, injured in your body, embarrassed about your body, or ashamed of your body. Just as Jesus was raised to life with a new and improved resurrection body, so we will follow him when he returns. We will be given new glorious, powerful, splendid resurrection bodies: never to get ill again; never to get injured again; never to be embarrassed about again; never to die again. Great news indeed!

The difference to death

Of course all this sounds good for our future, but does it change anything in the present? That's a good thing to think about. And the answer has to at least include that we face death differently from other people. We think about death differently; we don't have to avoid thinking and talking about death. Though we wish it on no-one, we do not fear it. We can see that what Paul says is true: to die is not the end. To die is gain because then we can be with Jesus, which is better by far. We have hope beyond this life. And we can say with confidence that the second after we breathe our last, we are in joyful fellowship with Jesus, only awaiting a glorious resurrection body when he comes again. We have already been raised to new life with Jesus, just as we already noted above from Colossians 3 and elsewhere. This new life in him continues even when our bodies fall asleep, give way and die. So we do not fear death because our life with Christ remains, and will only get better when we are 'clothed' with a new resurrection body upon Jesus' return.

This hope makes a difference to life as well, though. If a better and glorious life is to follow, we needn't obsess with getting the very best out of this life. Not that doing so would bring lasting happiness anyway, but the hope for a glorious resurrection with glorious resurrection bodies frees us from the frantic quest of the bucket list. It frees us from scampering through our days on this planet, desperately trying to squeeze in as many good experiences, great opportunities and noteworthy achievements as we can. It frees us to focus on others, putting their present and eternal needs before our own earthly desires, because we know the everlasting wonder that God has in store for us. This real hope makes all the difference.

Thinking about earthly desires versus eternal needs prepares us to consider the next question, that of judgement and the end of the world.

CHAPTER 4

The final judgement

Many of us have a basic problem these days coming to grips with the fact that there will be an end to the world. At the cosmic level, we're not entirely sure that there will be an end at all. But you can also hear it at a personal level, when young lovers talk about getting married and being with their new spouse *forever*. If they wanted to be precise, surely after the wedding they'd say they'll be with their spouse for 20 years, or 40 years, or 60 years. But you hear it all the time: "We are going to be together forever". To be fair, it's not a modern quandary at all. The world has always had an appearance of permanence. When King Solomon scribbled the Old Testament book of Ecclesiastes about 3,000 years ago, he said that the world appeared to just go on and on:

> Generations come and generations go, but the earth remains
> forever… The sun rises and the sun sets, and hurries back to where

it rises… What has been will be again, what has been done will be done again; there is nothing new under the sun. (Eccl 1:4, 5, 9)

Things just look like they'll never end.

I remember a TV commercial for a popular Australian beer, in which a man was on his couch watching TV and drinking a can of the advertised beer. And to his right appeared four riders on four horses—the four horsemen of the apocalypse from the book of Revelation, which some people think signal a final, cataclysmic battle between good and evil.[2] As they stand there at the edge of his TV room, dressed in all their fearful colours, his hysterical wife rushes into the living room and screams at her husband, "It's the four riders of the apocalypse". He just calmly responds, "Don't worry, it's not the end of the world", and resumes sipping his beer on the couch. It's a classic Australian take on everything in life.

But you don't have to be Australian to have an "It's not the end of the world" reaction to things in life. Even in response to the end of the world, you might shrug your shoulders and say it's not the end of the world. Our world has all the appearance of permanence. We think history is like the sun and wind, ever returning on its course, going round and round, never finishing.

The end of the world as we know it

But the basic problem with thinking that the world is permanent and that history is circular, forever going round and round, is that the Bible tells us that history is not like a circle but is like a line, heading to a final point or destination. There is an end; that is the consistent witness of Scripture. At times, in places like Daniel and Revelation, it is presented using vivid and dramatic symbolism and pictures. In other places it is spoken of in plain language. There are many things that are uncertain in our world, but you cannot mistake the clarity of the Bible's prediction of not just the end of the world, but also of the final judgement of all mankind at the time of the return of Jesus. Hebrews, for example, tells us that "people are destined to die once, and after that to face judgement" (9:27-28), before discussing the saving work of Christ.

Similarly, in Acts 17:30-31, the apostle Paul says to a gathered crowd of philosophers:

> "…[God] commands all people everywhere to repent. For he has set a day when he will judge the world with justice by the man he has appointed. He has given proof of this to everyone by raising him from the dead."

Things will not continue as they are forevermore. An end is coming: God has set a day of judgement for each person individually (as we learn from Hebrews 9), but also for the world in its totality. And you really must see that it's not merely a possibility, or even a probability. It is certain; it is definite. In the resurrection from the dead God showed his approval of Jesus to the entire universe and declared him to be Lord over life and death, and Judge of all things.

In fact, those two little verses in Acts 17, spoken to a group of intellectual heavyweights, many of whom laughed at the idea of resurrection from the dead, tell us some other important things about the final judgement. They tell us that the day of final judgement will be a day of justice. The world will be judged with justice. All the citizens of the earth will stand before the throne of Jesus to give account for how they lived their lives. It will be a time when people are judged according to what they've done (Rom 2:5-6), and when all deeds are taken into account, even the hidden thoughts and motives of the heart (Eccl 12:14). We'll explore how this plays out for the believer and the unbeliever shortly, because there are some critical differences. But the final judgement will be a time of justice.

The verses above also tell us about the identity of the judge whom God has appointed. It is Jesus, none other than the one who lived a perfectly obedient and sinless life and who died a painful death in the place of sinners like you and me. There will be an end, an end to the world as we know it, a final day of judgement, and it will be presided over by Jesus himself.

It will be an inescapable day of justice, with consequences for all those living on that day as well as everyone who has ever lived. We get a sense of its universal reach from as far back as the Old Testament book of Daniel, which foresees this:

> "Multitudes who sleep in the dust of the earth will awake: some
> to everlasting life, others to shame and everlasting contempt."
> (Dan 12:2)

Jesus himself says something very similar in John 5:28-29, the apostle Paul says something very similar in 2 Thessalonians 1:5-10, and in Revelation 20:11-15 the apostle John saw the grave give up those who had already died, and the sea return those who had drowned there, to the final judgement before the throne of Christ. All will rise from their resting place to be sorted according to the judgement of Jesus. As Jesus says in Matthew 25:

> "When the Son of Man comes in his glory, and all the angels
> with him, he will sit on his glorious throne. All the nations will

be gathered before him, and he will separate the people one from another… they will go away to eternal punishment, but the righteous to eternal life." (vv. 31-32, 46)

When Jesus returns everyone will rise from physical death for the final judgement, from which they will go to their eternal destinies. Jesus is the Judge and those who are righteous, that is who believe him wholeheartedly, go to eternal life with their new resurrection bodies (as we saw in the previous chapter). The final judgement for the believer is perhaps more like a final declaration; for those who trust in Jesus there is no uncertainty about where they will spend their eternity. Forgiveness, salvation and the payment of penalties all happened for believers when Jesus triumphed over sin, Satan and death with his own death and resurrection. The final judgement for those who have accepted Christ's death and resurrection in this life is like the decision of a judge in a case where there was never any doubt about the outcome.

So the final judgement is good news for believers. It is the time when Jesus declares with absolute clarity and finality the salvation he has won for us. There might be some reckoning of rewards to Christians in accordance with how they served their Master while he was away, which we'll discuss in a moment. But our eternal destiny with Christ in heaven is not in question.

Hell and the unbeliever

But what does the final judgement mean for unbelievers? What does it mean for those who consistently reject the good King and Judge Jesus for the duration of their life, whether in anger and hostility, or in ignorance and indifference? The New Testament straightforwardly says that those who reject Jesus in their earthly life will be cast out from his goodness and blessing for eternity. In a very real sense, if you resist relationship with God through Jesus in this life then God won't force that upon you for eternity.

In the same way as when a believer dies, an unbeliever's body rots in the ground or otherwise decays and decomposes. But unlike the believer, whose soul is joined in joyful fellowship with Jesus the second after they breathe their final breath, the unbeliever appears to experience some form of intermediate punishment after physical death but before the final judgement. In the parable of the rich man and Lazarus in Luke 16, the rich man who showed Jesus and others no charity in his earthly life appears in torment in Hades,[3] which was thought of as a shadowy and probably temporary resting place of the dead. It's worth remembering that Jesus is speaking in a parable in these verses, and the point he is trying to make is about responding to the promise of God's word in this lifetime, whilst there is still time. So perhaps we should be careful in saying anything too definitive about what unbelievers experience between physical death and final judgement from this passage.

But if there's any mystery about what exactly happens to unbelievers in this intermediate stage, the New Testament is not vague at all about their final destiny. As difficult as it is to say and write these words, as offensive as they are to some modern ears, and as personally grievous as it might be when we think about our unbelieving friends and family, hell is the final destiny of those who reject Jesus. At the last judgement, an unbeliever's body and soul will once again be reunited to stand before Christ's throne. They will hear his declaration that hell is their final destiny because of their rejection of Jesus and his ways. Christians say this with tears in their eyes and no glee in their hearts, and not because we think we are in any way superior to others, but only because Jesus spoke about hell more than anyone else, mentioning it 11 of the 12 times it appears in the New Testament.

Despite popular opinion and AC/DC lyrics, hell won't be a party or a happy reunion and it won't be good. "Friends might be there too",[4] but that will offer no consolation. It is vitally important for us to hear the New Testament's description of that fate as everlasting destruction (2 Thess 1:9). The New Testament *paints a picture* of it as eternal darkness, or an ever-burning fire, a place of weeping and gnashing of teeth (Matt 18:8-9; 22:13; 24:51; 25:30, 41; 2 Pet 2:17; Jude 1:7; Rev 20:14-15). So whatever hell *actually* turns out to be—presumably, the Bible paints these pictures because plain words cannot convey the horror—hell is something that is real and awful and avoidable only by turning and trusting in Jesus. This means that for all people who are not yet believers in Christ, there is nothing more important to consider than their eternal destiny.

Rewards in heaven

So there are two entirely contrasting fates at the final judgement of Jesus: one for the believer and one for the unbeliever. It will be a time of great joy for the believer, and of unimaginable pain for the unbeliever. As we noted above, the salvation of the wholehearted believer will not be in doubt at the final judgement, because Jesus absorbed the penalty for our sin and rebellion when he died on the cross in our place.

But this wonderful fact might lead Christians into a faulty way of thinking. Some might think that if their sins are paid for in Christ's death, and if their salvation is guaranteed, then what they do with their life doesn't count. You might think it doesn't matter whether you obey or disobey God; or that what you do with the gifts, talents, and opportunities God gives you to put into his service is of little consequence. I'd be worried if this was your way of thinking; it would make me question whether you really understood the cost of the salvation Christ purchased for you with his blood. I'd wonder whether perhaps you still thought that the world's ways were better than God's way for our lives, and I'd have doubts that you genuinely counted the cost of being a disciple of Christ. I'd wonder whether you realized that we were raised to new life in Christ the moment we became believers, and I'd be unsure whether you understood that having been raised to new life in him, we set our minds and hearts and lives upon things above rather than on worldly things below (as the apostle Paul puts it in Colossians 3:1-4).

Sure—we don't obey or serve God to earn, deserve or merit our salvation; we obey and serve God *as a response* to the salvation he gives us in Christ, and because we love him. But what we do with our lives still matters to him. It will be reckoned, judged, taken into account. We've seen this already, in chapter 2 with the parable of the talents. In other places, Jesus talks about rewards in heaven. In Matthew 6, Jesus contrasts the deeds done by Pharisees for the approval of men with what he desires from his followers, which is that they live for God's approval. It's interesting to see how he appeals to his listeners: he says that if you do your acts of righteousness to be seen by other people, "you will have no reward from your Father in heaven" (Matt 6:1). From what we know in the remainder of Scripture, the reward in heaven Jesus speaks about here cannot be our salvation, otherwise he'd be saying that we can earn our salvation by giving to the needy, or praying or fasting, so long as we don't do it publicly.

Rather, Christians who live righteous lives and who do good deeds as an expression of their faith in Christ and love for God will receive some other kind of reward from God in heaven. What we do in this life will be taken into account, and we should use the gifts, talents, time, possessions and opportunities that God has given us for his service. Talking to Christians in Corinth, the apostle Paul says:

> For we must all appear before the judgement seat of Christ, so that each one may receive what is due us for the things done while in the body, whether good or bad. (2 Cor 5:10)

Paul will later say in 1 Timothy 5:25 that good deeds, even ones that are not obvious, will not remain hidden forever but will be brought to light by the final judgement of God. And Hebrews 4:13 reminds us that this can work both ways. The Christian need not fear a destiny of eternal destruction, but our deeds will still be brought to light, whether good or bad. We will feel the weight of our disobedience, even if that is in a way that won't continue in or detract from our experience of eternal life. We cannot fail to realize that our lives are precious opportunities to serve God in ways that will not go unnoticed and unrewarded.

We cannot say for sure what these rewards will be, and Scripture offers no indication that any believer's experience of heaven will be deficient in any way, either by remembering their personal sin or by envying the rewards of other believers. Perhaps the rewards spoken of will be greater responsibility in the life to come. Perhaps it will just be the knowledge that there are people in heaven who are there at least partly because of our efforts in care and evangelism (e.g. Paul describes the Thessalonian Christians as "our hope, our joy, or the crown in which we will glory in the presence of the Lord Jesus when he comes" (1 Thess 2:19). For myself, I can think of nothing more rewarding than hearing the voice of Jesus greet me with those beautiful words,

"Well done, good and faithful servant… Come and share in your master's happiness!" (Matt 25:23).

The difference to now

The final judgement draws our thoughts towards the end of time. It cannot help but make us think about then. But it also makes us think about now; it changes the way we think about life. When we know that there will be a final judgement, we are forced to recognize that this life is not all there is; and yet we know that this life is the time when our actions, our beliefs, our decisions and our loyalties determine where we spend eternity. In the movie *Gladiator*, Russell Crowe's character says, "What we do in life echoes in eternity". He meant something different than what I've been talking about, but he was right. We only have this life to ensure that we are with Jesus in heaven for eternity by wholeheartedly believing in him now. Once our bodies die, our fate is sealed and will be proclaimed with absolute clarity by Jesus at the final judgement. This life is not all there is, which means we can go easy on the plastic surgery. But this life is it in terms of squaring up your eternal destiny, and so we really do need to think hard, investigate thoroughly, choose wisely, and stay the course.

This has obvious implications for our godliness, which we'll talk more about in our final chapter. It also has clear consequences for evangelism, as we urgently hold out the offer of life in Jesus to our friends, our classmates, our family, our teachers and our co-workers. The final judgement at the return of Jesus also means that we need not become obsessed or preoccupied with any injustice we might suffer. Not that we are dismissive of all injustices, but we can let go of some of the occasions in which we are wronged. And we certainly need not become absorbed with a desire for revenge—because we know that Jesus will judge justly at the final judgement when all things are brought to light.

What we do in life echoes in eternity. As we saw last chapter, if we're with Jesus in this life then our souls will be with him the very second we die, and we'll then await our glorious resurrection bodies when he returns. But if we reject him in this life, he will reject us for all eternity. And that is not a welcome future. This life is not all there is, and knowing this changes the way we think about our life and the choices we make: who we'll follow, what we'll do, and what we won't do.

CHAPTER 5

Eternal Life

Eternity is a long time. And here on Earth, nothing that goes on for a long time is really positive in our experience. We even have the saying, "You can have too much of a good thing". So having a good thing eternally, even something as positive as life, can seem disconcerting. We might wonder, "What am I going to do for all that time?" It can be hard to imagine what eternal life will be like. Part of the problem is just the way we think about eternal life, as if it is some kind of floaty, airy existence. Part of it is that our best approximations are pretty lame actually. For example, there's an ice cream called 'Heaven on a Stick'—is that really the closest comparison we can come up with? I mean ice cream is good, but really? Or there's rugby, which has often been called the game they play in heaven, though I'm not quite sure why given that it's only played in a handful of countries. But putting that aside, does rugby really match up to eternity in heaven? Or there's the well-known old-school song by Bryan Adams called 'Heaven', which was remixed more recently by someone called DJ Sammy:

> Baby, you're all that I want, when you're lyin' here in my arms
> I'm findin' it hard to believe we're in heaven
> And love is all that I need and I found it there in your heart
> It isn't too hard to see we're in heaven.[5]

Romance might seem more apt than rugby, but is that what eternal life will really be like—romance, rugby and ice cream? That's the question we are considering in this chapter. Previously, we discovered that when our bodies pass away we live on with Jesus and we await glorious, new resurrection bodies when Jesus returns. But what will eternal life be like, with Jesus, in our new skin? That's the question for now.

Eternal life with God

The first thing we must understand is that 'heaven' is primarily about eternal life *with God*. It's about being in relationship with God. Chances are that if we don't think of heaven as ice cream or romance, we think it will be like a beautiful tropical island—sort of like the best earthly experience imaginable, just amplified or magnified. But in the last couple of chapters in the Bible there are glorious visions or pictures of eternal life. They are descriptions of what it *is* like, rather than what it *looks* like, if you can get that distinction; but they are glorious no less. This is what the apostle John saw:

> Then I saw a "new heaven and a new earth", for the first heaven and the first earth had passed away, and there was no longer any sea. I saw the Holy City, the new Jerusalem, coming down out of heaven from God, prepared as a bride beautifully dressed for her husband. And I heard a loud voice from the throne saying, "Look! God's dwelling place is now among the people, and he will dwell with them. They will be his people, and God himself will be with them and be their God. 'He will wipe every tear from their eyes. There will be no more death' or mourning or crying or pain, for the old order of things has passed away." (Rev 21:1-4)

So the new creation is a place, a real place. The opening line of the Bible tells us that "In the beginning God created the heavens and the earth"—that is, he created the entire universe, or what this little passage calls "the first heaven and the first earth". And in many important ways, the opening chapters of the Bible give us as many clues about our eternal home as the closing chapters. That's because life eternal will be spent in a renewed and restored creation. The first creation will be transformed into a new creation, the first heavens and earth giving way to a new heavens and new earth. What God did the first time he will do again into eternity. This makes perfect sense too: if he moulded such a wondrous physical universe the first time around, he's hardly likely to junk it all in favour of a weird, disembodied ghost land.

Of course the new creation will not be exactly the same as the world we now know, any more than Jesus' resurrection body was exactly the same as his earthly body. The point is that creation as we know it will be resolved, not dissolved; renewed, not removed. And this makes sense; if we're going to have glorious resurrection bodies then they'll need some kind of 'space' or 'place' to inhabit. So it follows that not only will our bodies be resurrected, the creation they inhabit will also be renewed. At the end of all things, after Jesus has returned, after the final judgement, there will be new heavens and a new earth. A new creation, a renewed physical place.

Nevertheless, notice that the emphasis here is not so much on what that place is like but on who will be in that place. The focus is less upon it being like a Caribbean beach resort and more about our relationship with God. It's not that it won't be a ripper place, but the highlight is that it will be the dwelling place of God among his people. They will be his people, and God himself will be with them and will be their God. According to our Scriptures, at the moment heaven is the place where God dwells, and the earth is the place where we live. But the heavens and the earth shall be renewed, purified and made perfect, so that there is no further separation between Earth and the dwelling place of God. They shall be one at last. And God takes the initiative in bridging that gap. He will come down from 'heaven' to dwell with men and women in a renewed and unified creation. We will be *his* people.

Being reunited with God is good news for us because relationships are the very heart and nucleus of life. Relationships are what we all like talking about the most—who likes who, and whether the first who is liked back by the second who, and all that kind of stuff. If we are honest with ourselves, the prettiest beach in the world is an awful place to spend any length of time if you're there by yourself, cut off from everyone else. This just shows that relationships are the things that really count. So, naturally, when the Bible pictures eternal life the emphasis is less on the place and more on the relationship between God and his people. It's a relationship that will be marked by the absence of sorrow and pain; a relationship of tender, personal care; and a relationship that will not be broken by death, as even death has been destroyed in the final judgement (see Revelation 20:14).

This also makes sense of hell. We've already noted that most of us think of hell as though it were some cartoon place with fire and brimstone and a little devil character running around poking people in the butt with a pitchfork. But in truth, hell is the experience of enduring the righteous anger of God and being cut off from his grace and favour. In hell, the person in charge is not the devil but God, because the devil likewise is judged with eternal destruction. If hell is really about being cut off from relationship with God, and being removed from his grace and favour, then effectively it means that people who throughout their lives persistently reject relationship with God through Jesus will be given what they ask for—for all eternity. That is to say, if you don't want friendship with God in this life then he won't force that upon you for eternity in the life to come. And it's absolutely critical to recognize that being cut off from relationship with God means being cut off from the source and giver of all good things. It means being unable to access his grace and favour; it means forgoing forgiveness and instead receiving what you deserve for what you have done in this life. It means you won't live with the one who will wipe away every tear from the eyes of his people. It means you won't dwell with the God who will ensure there is no more death or pain.

That is the real thrust of the way the Bible thinks of 'heaven'— eternal life with God. Whenever we think of heaven as a beach or a cosmic Disneyland, or as being about fun or being reunited with believing friends and relations or whatever it might be, we miss the force of Scripture, which says that the best thing will be life eternal with God. To be frank, if God is not there then the prettiest beach will be hell. And if God is there, then the ugliest ghetto or desert wasteland will still be bliss. Life eternal with God will be *that* good.

An improvement upon Eden

And, in point of fact, we can say with confidence that the new creation won't be the ugliest ghetto or desert wasteland, because it will be an improvement upon Eden. We saw earlier how the opening verses of the Bible give us many clues about our eternal home. But as it turns out, the new creation will be better than the first creation; even better than Eden, where the first humans lived in relationship with God before sin entered the world. Look at the final depiction of eternal life in the last chapter of the Bible, as seen by the apostle John:

Then the angel showed me the river of the water of life, as clear as crystal, flowing from the throne of God and of the Lamb down the middle of the great street of the city. On each side of the river stood the tree of life, bearing twelve crops of fruit, yielding its fruit every month. And the leaves of the tree are for the healing of the nations. No longer will there be any curse. The throne of God and of the Lamb will be in the city, and his servants will serve him. They will see his face, and his name will be on their foreheads. There will be no more night. They will not need the light of a lamp or the light of the sun, for the Lord God will give them light. And they will reign for ever and ever. (Rev 22:1-5)

As we saw earlier, in Revelation 21, our eternal destination appears to be a perfect city, "the new Jerusalem" depicted in all its dazzling glory and bejewelled splendour, coming down from heaven to earth. But as that chapter progresses it's hard to work out whether the picture of the perfect city is really describing a place we will inhabit or whether it's using that picture to describe what we will be like as the perfected people of God. Perhaps those two ideas merge in that single image, and perhaps that's the point. But when we get to Revelation 22 we see a familiar picture, because it's the picture of a garden within that great city; it's a vision of a new and improved Eden.

The whole idea of improvement sounds positive to us because the word 'improvement' basically means that something is getting better. Better performance, better quality, better results. At least, improvements are *meant* to mean that things get better, although they don't always work out as planned. The new operating system for your phone or computer may lose some of the features of the old system that you really liked. The term 'home improvements' reminds me of the picture I saw of a new balcony added to an apartment in some suave European city. It looked like a great addition until you realized that the balcony sat about a metre above a set of train tracks. So it wasn't going to have a great view to start with. And then the 10:57 freight train from Vladivostok or Warsaw was going to smash that balcony to smithereens. Sometimes improvements don't actually make things better.

But we can have a much higher degree of confidence in the new and improved Eden we see in Revelation 22. Some things look very familiar. The tree of life is there, somehow stretching over both banks of the river of the water of life, providing food and healing all year round. There will be no shortages, no off-seasons where anyone has to do without. Eternal life with God means a life of abundance, forever.

But just as remarkable as the tree that *is* there is the tree that *isn't* there. You may remember from back in Genesis 2 that in the garden of Eden there was another tree, the tree of the knowledge of good and evil. In the first garden it functioned as a tree of temptation; a temptation that the first humans found too difficult to resist. But in the new heavens and the new earth there is no tree of temptation; it is not present. The devil will be destroyed with finality, our sinful natures will be perfected, and there will be no more temptation. None of the things that bring sin and misery into this creation will be present in the next. There will be no repeat of the fall of man into sin and death.

So there will be no curse. In the earliest chapters of the Bible we are told that after our first parents disobeyed God, they were shut out from the garden of Eden, they were shut out from the tree of life, and they were shut out from unbroken fellowship with God. That result was called 'the curse'. And in the following chapters of Scripture, and in human history, we see that curse played out predictably countless times. Humans blame each other and struggle with each other. And we struggle with creation, having to work hard to stay alive. But in heaven there will be no curse. No battle with creation, no battle with each other, and no broken relationship with God. The throne of God and the throne of the Lamb (that's Jesus) will be there, and we will see Jesus' face. And we will share in his victory and triumph and reign over all things forever. We look forward to a new and improved Eden, even better than the Eden in the first creation God made.

Training for eternity

The Bible's vision for eternity is a wonderful picture indeed. But it raises two important questions in my mind, and perhaps also in yours. The first is: If it will be as good as it sounds, then what is God waiting for—why has he taken so long to bring it all into effect? And the second question is: How do we prepare for the new heavens and the new earth?

The answer to these questions can be found in the last words we have from the apostle Peter:

> But do not forget this one thing, dear friends: With the Lord a day is like a thousand years, and a thousand years are like a day. The Lord is not slow in keeping his promise, as some understand slowness. Instead he is patient with you, not wanting anyone to perish, but everyone to come to repentance.

But the day of the Lord will come like a thief. The heavens will disappear with a roar; the elements will be destroyed by fire, and the earth and everything done in it will be laid bare.

Since everything will be destroyed in this way, what kind of people ought you to be? You ought to live holy and godly lives as you look forward to the day of God and speed its coming. That day will bring about the destruction of the heavens by fire, and the elements will melt in the heat. But in keeping with his promise we are looking forward to a new heaven and a new earth, where righteousness dwells. (2 Pet 3:8-13)

It's a terrific passage, and in some ways a terrifying one. The day of the Lord, the return of Jesus, the "destruction"[6] or passing of the first heavens and earth to make way for a renewed, purified and improved heaven and earth, is so long coming only because God is patient. He is not preoccupied with other things and he hasn't forgotten about us here on planet Earth. God is patient and he wants to give as many people as possible, and perhaps this includes you, a chance to repent (that is, an opportunity to turn back and trust in him). If you haven't repented—turned back to trust in him—it is something worth doing as a matter of priority and urgency. And for those who have turned back to trust in God, who is patient, it wouldn't be out of order for us to be patient in response. If God has been so patient with us, we can wait for him to have his way with the world he made.

Actually, these words instruct us to look forward to the day of God and to look forward to the new heaven and new earth. So part of the way we prepare for the return of Christ and the coming of the new heaven and new earth is to look forward to it all, to eagerly expect it (which is the idea behind "speed its coming"). If we anticipate it eagerly, and get ourselves involved in activities that anticipate the new creation (like godly living and proclaiming Jesus to our world), perhaps that will bring the day of the Lord forward, as those whom God is waiting to bring into his eternal kingdom are ushered in with the help of our actions, words and lives. Or perhaps it will just seem in our minds that the day of the Lord, the return of Jesus, is rushing towards us. Most of us get absorbed in the things of this world, things that will be destroyed when the old order of things passes away, when the first creation melts in preparation for the hope that the new heavens and new earth will bring. But for as long as God's patience means there is still time, we ought to turn back to him and, having turned back, be eagerly anticipating the new creation, saying in our minds and with our lives, "Speed the day"!

In major league baseball in America there is a phenomenon known as spring training. It is a series of practice and exhibition games before the start of the regular season. Spring training starts in mid-February and continues right up until the opening day of the baseball season, which is traditionally in the first week of April. Spring training allows new players to try out for spots on the regular team, and it gives regular team players some practice time prior to the regular season, when every game counts. Team members normally wear their batting practice uniforms for the length of spring training and will only don their normal jerseys once the season proper has begun.

These verses in 2 Peter 3 tell us that as we look forward to the coming of the day of the Lord, the sudden and unexpected return of Jesus; and as we look forward to the coming of the new heavens and earth, the renewed creation, where God will dwell with his people in perfection; our lives here are like spring training.[7] Given that everything will be destroyed and the new creation is coming, the apostle Peter asks, "What sort of lives should we live?" And his answer is that we should live holy and godly lives, as if we're in spring training for our eternity. Our earthly bodies are like training jerseys that we wear in this life, in this creation, while we prepare for eternity in the new creation with our resurrection bodies. We are getting ready for the main game that starts when Jesus returns.

So it is appropriate to ask yourself whether you are in spring training when it comes to what you talk about and the way you talk about it. Is what you do with your time and your energy and your money and your body the output of a holy and godly life, the life of someone preparing for eternity in perfection with God? Is the thing that you are most concerned about—finding the right boyfriend or perhaps just any boyfriend, getting the right grades, taking the right next step along the right career path, squeezing in as much fun as possible, never missing out on a good opportunity for yourself or your family—is this a reflection of the fact that Jesus could come at any moment, like a thief in the night? Do your daily decisions reflect a knowledge that nothing really lasts forever other than personal godliness, and that the basic elements of this creation will melt down in preparation for the coming of a new, restored, perfect and eternal creation where we will live with God forever?

If you ask yourself those questions and the answer is "Yessir, I'm in training. Batter up!" then let me encourage you to keep going.

But if you look at those questions and it really does seem to you like you're absorbed just a little too much in a world that is temporary and passing, then don't just notice it and do nothing. Action, new decisions, or recalibrated thinking are required.

It's not necessarily easy to follow through on these things, but it's easy enough to understand that we pursue holy and godly lives as we look forward to the day of God; as we look forward to the new creation; as we anticipate our new home of righteousness. Our new home will not really be like ice cream, or rugby, or even romance. It will be life eternal with God, in a new and improved Eden, where there is no temptation, no more pain and no more curse, and where we will see his face.

I hope this book has persuaded you to say in your mind, in your heart and with your life, "Speed that day!"

Endnotes

1   I think it's better to label the future that we look forward to as
    Christians as 'eternal life' rather than 'heaven', just because when
    you say 'heaven' people think you're talking about floating around
    in the sky somewhere rather than eternal life with God in a renewed
    creation. There's more about this in the final chapter.
2   I think this is a shoddy misreading of that part of Revelation, which
    fails to take into consideration not only that Revelation is highly
    symbolic but also that it describes in symbolic ways things that are
    happening right now, in between the resurrection and return of Jesus.
    Anyway…
3   Some Bibles translate 'Hades' in Luke 16:23 as 'hell', but it seems
    unlikely that we're meant to understand this as the final place of
    judgement.
4   A Young, M Young and B Scott, 'Highway to Hell', from the album
    Highway to Hell, Atlantic Records, London, 1979.
5   B Adams and J Vallance, 'Heaven', from the album *Reckless*, A&M
    Records, New York, 1983.
6   "Destruction" here cannot mean the total obliteration of the creation.
    Peter uses the same word to discuss the destruction of the world by

water in Noah's time (2 Pet 3:6), and clearly the world was not totally vaporized at that time, although there was a pretty comprehensive wipe-out of humanity and all its works. So it seems Peter is using the word here to refer to a thorough and destructive judgement that prepares for a new creation.

7   Obviously, this is just an illustration that cannot be stretched too far. For example, it is not the case that, as in spring training, you either do or don't make the team based on your performance. The point is that, as in spring training, you are preparing for a future reality.

Feedback on this resource

If you enjoyed this Little Black Book, you might like to use the Facebook page as an easy way to let your friends know about it (as well as the other books in the series). And feel free to use the Facebook page to give me your feedback, comments and suggestions for future topics.

www.facebook.com/littleblackbooks

Matthias Media is an evangelical publishing ministry that seeks to persuade all Christians of the truth of God's purposes in Jesus Christ as revealed in the Bible, and equip them with high-quality resources, so that by the work of the Holy Spirit they will:

- abandon their lives to the honour and service of Christ in daily holiness and decision-making
- pray constantly in Christ's name for the fruitfulness and growth of his gospel
- speak the Bible's life-changing word whenever and however they can—in the home, in the world and in the fellowship of his people.

Our resources range from Bible studies and books through to training courses, audio sermons and children's Sunday School material. To find out more, and to access samples and free downloads, visit our website:

www.matthiasmedia.com

How to buy our resources

1. Direct from us over the internet:
   – in the US: www.matthiasmedia.com
   – in Australia: www.matthiasmedia.com.au

2. Direct from us by phone: please visit our website for current phone contact information.

3. Through a range of outlets in various parts of the world. Visit **www.matthiasmedia.com/contact** for details about recommended retailers in your part of the world, including www.thegoodbook.co.uk in the United Kingdom.

4. Trade enquiries can be addressed to:
   – in the US and Canada: sales@matthiasmedia.com
   – in Australia and the rest of the world: sales@matthiasmedia.com.au

5. Visit **GoThereFor.com** for subscription-based access to a great-value range of digital resources.

Register at our website for our **free** regular email update to receive information about the latest new resources, **exclusive special offers**, and free articles to help you grow in your Christian life and ministry.

MORE
· Little Black Books ·
books that get to the point

FOR MORE INFORMATION OR TO ORDER CONTACT:

Matthias Media
Email: sales@matthiasmedia.com.au
www.matthiasmedia.com.au

Matthias Media (USA)
Email: sales@matthiasmedia.com
www.matthiasmedia.com

Right Side Up

"I set out to write a book for new Christians, to explain what it means to be a Christian and what the lifelong adventure of following Jesus is like. But I soon realized that what Jesus wants to say to a new Christian is really the same thing he wants to keep saying to the seasoned saint: "Whoever loses his life for my sake will find it". My prayer is that this book will persuade you of the truth of those words, and help you live like you believe them. It's a book for the brand new Christian that should challenge every believer—whether you've been following Jesus for five minutes or fifty years."

—Author, Paul Grimmond

Hanging in There

Hanging in There is a book about God, you, the Bible, prayer, church, relationships, sex, feelings, doubts, love and, above all, hanging in there as a Christian. If you're a young Christian (teenager to early 20s), new to the Christian faith or a long-serving Christian who could use some encouragement, this book is for you.

Short Steps for Long Gains: Youth Edition

Adopting the successful Bible discussion model of *Short Steps for Long Gains* and *Short Steps for Long Gains: Family Edition*, this new addition to the series will get helpful Christian discussion going with teenagers. Each study is brief, and by no means covers everything you could say on the topic. But sometimes, short steps, even for little feet, are the best way to make long gains.

- 26 short Bible discussions for parents or youth leaders to do with teenagers.
- Important and interesting range of topics: from A for Assurance through to Z for Zeal, with lots of stops along the way, including G for Gossip, L for Loneliness and S for Sex.